T0040142

Reflections for My Baby

AN ILLUSTRATED KEEPSAKE JOURNAL TO RECORD MEDITATIONS AND MILESTONES DURING YOUR BABY'S FIRST YEAR OF LIFE

This journal was given with gratitude to my child

_____

born

_____

by your loving mother

_____

Reflections for My Baby

AN ILLUSTRATED KEEPSAKE JOURNAL TO RECORD MEDITATIONS AND MILESTONES DURING YOUR BABY'S FIRST YEAR OF LIFE

Laura Buller

Bluestreak
BOOKS

Bluestreak
an imprint of Weldon Owen International
PO Box 3088 San Rafael, CA 94912
www.weldonowen.com

© 2021 Weldon Owen

All rights reserved, including the right of
reproduction in whole or in part in any form.

Library of Congress Cataloging in Publication data is available.

Printed in China

ISBN-13: 978-1-68188-704-3

10 9 8 7 6 5 4 3 2 1

Contents

INTRODUCTION 7

CHAPTER ONE: COMING SOON 11

CHAPTER TWO: WELCOME TO THE WORLD 23

CHAPTER THREE: FAMILY TIMES 39

CHAPTER FOUR: A DAY IN THE LIFE 51

CHAPTER FIVE: EXPLORING AND LEARNING 75

CHAPTER SIX: HOPES AND DREAMS 91

INTRODUCTION

Becoming a parent is an unforgettable experience. The excitement at finding out the news. The sleepless nights when it all became real. The wonder of the first ultrasound scan. The pleasures and pitfalls of pregnancy. The indescribable joy of birth, and of seeing your tiny face. And . . . back to the sleepless nights. But as much as I want to remember everything, it's hard to take it all in. So I'm collecting all my thoughts in this journal. I want to remember it all—from your first gummy smile to the way I felt when watching you sleep. Then, I want to share it with you. The story of your early life is all your own. Little reminders on these pages prompt my memories, and there is a secret place at the back of the book to make a time capsule for you. As the song says, you are my sunshine, and this is for you.

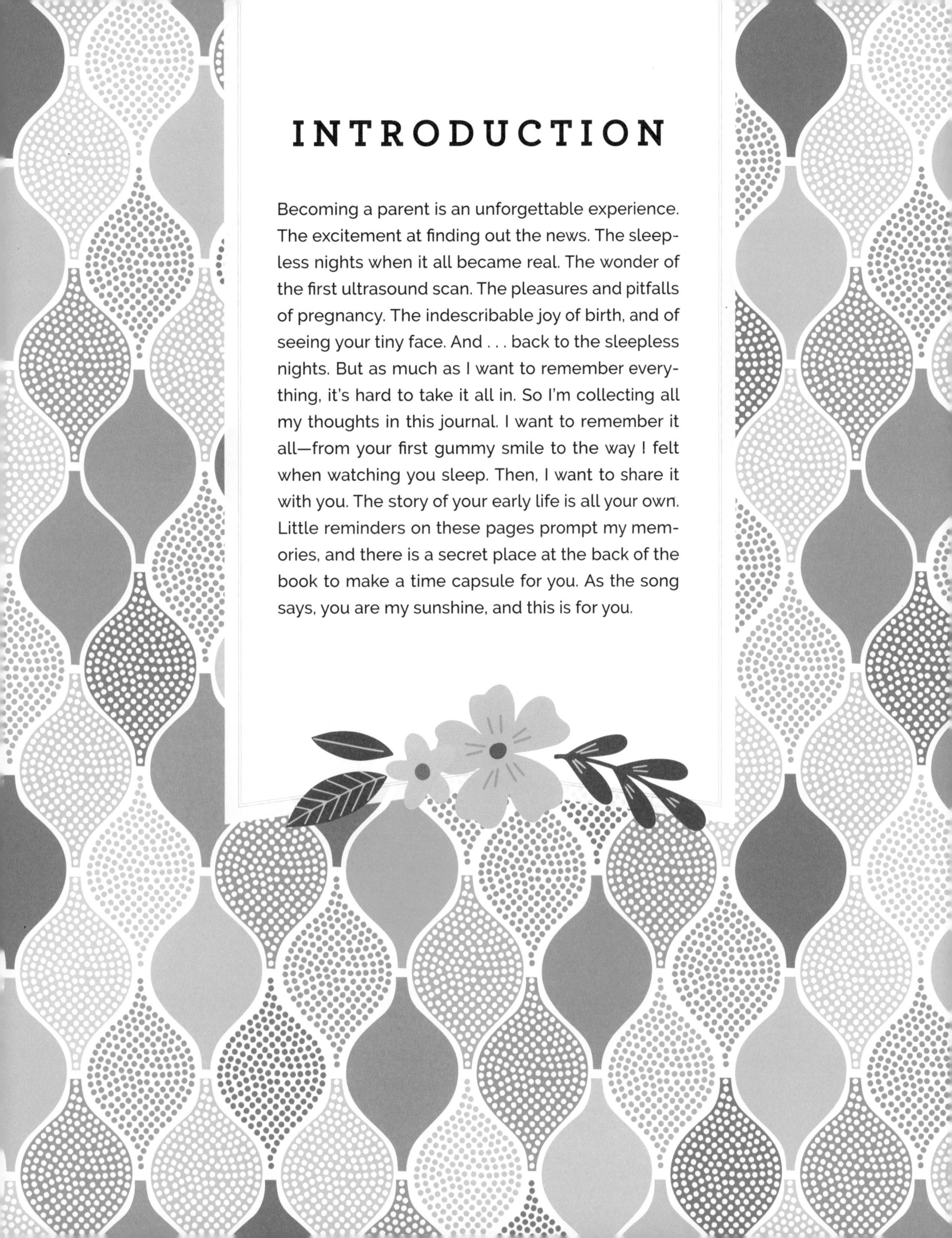

A LETTER TO MY CHILD, FROM MY HEART TO YOURS

Written on _____

As I write this, I am in _____

CHAPTER ONE

Coming Soon

GETTING READY FOR A NEW ARRIVAL

EXPECTING

Life is always a rich and steady time when you are waiting for something to happen or to hatch.

– E. B. WHITE

This is when and where I found out I was expecting you _____

_____

_____

_____

_____

_____

_____

My emotions were _____

_____

_____

_____

_____

_____

_____

_____

My partner felt

I shared the news with everyone by

I couldn't wait to meet you because

A NEW LEAF ON THE FAMILY TREE

A baby is God's opinion that life should go on.

– CARL SANDBURG

My family reacted to the news about you by _____

_____

_____

_____

_____

_____

Other children in the family said _____

_____

_____

_____

_____

_____

_____

_____

_____

I celebrated with the family by

A family member I bonded with at that time was

One of the sweetest or funniest things a family member said about the news was

PREPARING FOR A LITTLE ONE

A mother's joy begins when new life is stirring inside . . . when a tiny heartbeat is heard for the very first time.

– UNKNOWN

Some of the things I did to get ready were _____

_____

_____

_____

_____

_____

The first thing I bought was _____

_____

_____

_____

_____

_____

_____

_____

My circle of friends helped me by

My friends gave me this advice

US TOGETHER

Pregnancy is getting company inside one's skin.

– MAGGIE SCARF

My pregnancy felt _____

_____

_____

_____

_____

The best part was _____

_____

_____

_____

_____

The hardest part was _____

_____

_____

_____

_____

I didn't expect

When I first felt you move or kick it was

We went everywhere together—including

These are the sounds and voices you heard

LITTLE WISHES

Babies . . . are like little bundles of hope.
Like the future in a basket.

– LISH MCBRIDE

These are the features or traits I hoped to pass down to you

And my dreams for what kind of parent I would become

I was ready for my life to change because

What motherhood meant to me

As your due date got closer, I felt

CHAPTER TWO

Welcome to the World

YOUR FIRST DAYS

HAPPY BIRTHDAY

Childbirth is more admirable than conquest, more amazing than self-defense, and as courageous as either one.

– GLORIA STEINEM

You were born on _____

_____

At (time) _____

_____

In _____

_____

And I named you _____

_____

I knew you were ready for the world when _____

_____

_____

_____

_____

_____

_____

These were the plans I had for your birth

My feelings on the big day (or night!) were

My partner was feeling

Something funny that I remember was

One thing I didn't expect was

Here is the story of how we met for the very first time

YOUR FIRST DAY

There are places in the heart you don't even know exist until you love a child.

– ANNE LAMOTT

I finally got to see you. You looked _____

I was surprised by _____

I dressed you in

When I looked at you or held you, I felt

My partner felt

This is how you spent your first hours

Something about you I found amazing right away was

I was grateful for

When I was feeding you, I thought

The story of your first night

A FAMILY WELCOME

A baby is born with a need to be loved—and never outgrows it.

– FRANK A. CLARK

Your first family visitor (or visitors) was _____

_____

_____

_____

_____

_____

Other family members and friends who stopped by were _____

_____

_____

_____

_____

_____

_____

_____

_____

Here are some of the things they said

Some of the gifts they brought were

I was particularly happy when

SWEET STORIES

The littlest feet make the biggest footprints in our hearts.

– UNKNOWN

Here are some memories about your first few days

COMING HOME

Loving a baby is a circular business, kind of a feedback loop. The more you give the more you get and the more you get the more you feel like giving.

– PENELOPE LEACH

I brought you home on _____

_____

_____

I'd describe the first days as _____

_____

_____

_____

_____

_____

_____

_____

_____

_____

_____

I felt happiest when

Some of the tough parts were

People who helped were

It was all worth it when

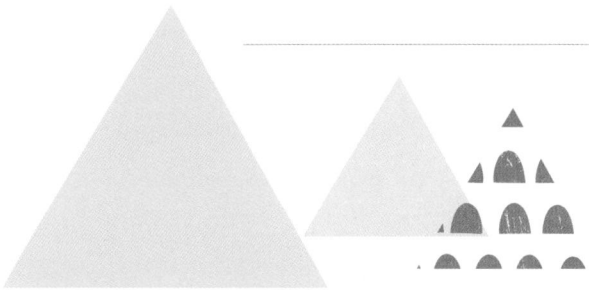

CHAPTER THREE

Family Times

HOME TOGETHER

A HAPPY HOUSE

A baby makes love stronger, the days shorter, the nights longer, savings smaller, and a home happier.

– UNKNOWN

This is where we lived when you were a baby

Here's who lived in the house with you

We had a pet called

You slept in

That room was special because

MOMMY AND ME

The life of a mother is the life of a child:
you are two blossoms on a single branch.

– KAREN MAEZEN MILLER

Here is a letter to you about my feelings and experiences during the first few weeks of being your mother

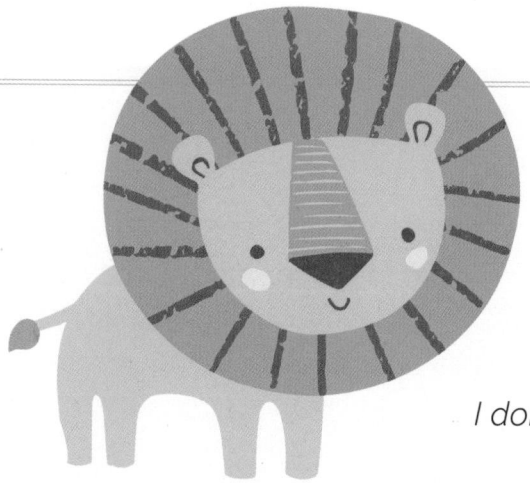

YOUR VIPs

I don't know why they say you have a baby.
The baby has you.

– GALLAGHER

Important adults in your babyhood were _____

_____

_____

_____

_____

_____

You adored _____

_____

_____

_____

_____

_____

_____

_____

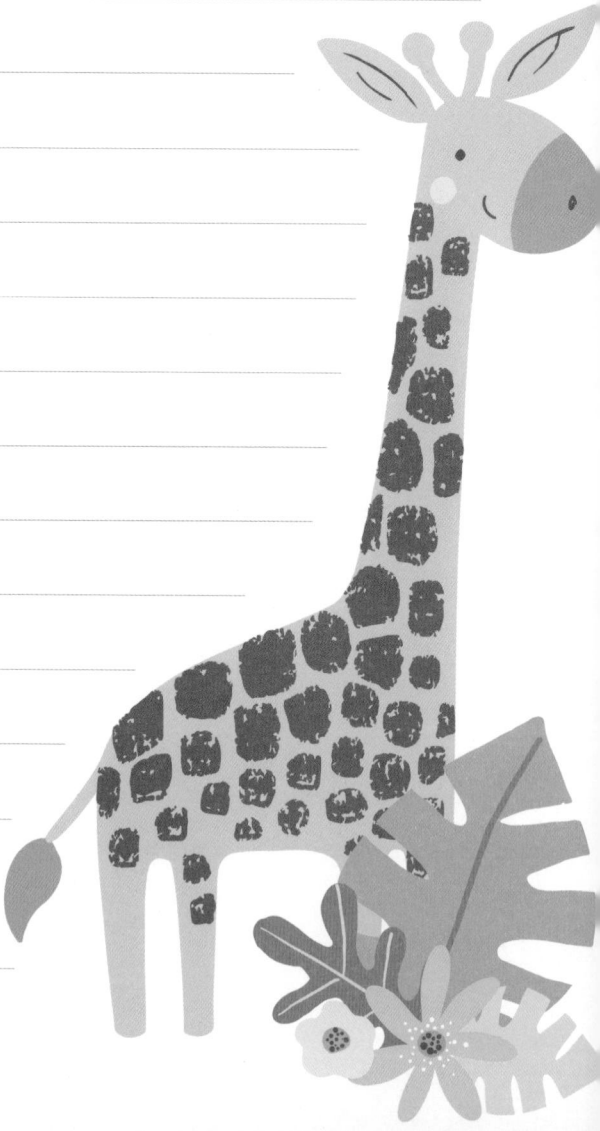

You were always comforted by a cuddle from

Someone who made you giggle was

Here's a memory of when you met your grandparent(s)

CELEBRATING WITH YOU

A new baby is like the beginning of all things . . .
wonder, hope, a dream of possibilities.

– EDA J. LESHAN

I celebrated your arrival by _____

_____

_____

_____

_____

_____

_____

Some of the family traditions I hoped to carry on with you were _____

_____

_____

_____

_____

_____

_____

And new traditions I wanted to start were

This is how I ended each day with you

Your first family celebration was

When you were together with my whole family, I felt

Something you did that made people smile

The first birthday party you went to was

The holiday we most enjoyed together was

Some of my best memories were

Some of your special holiday outfits were

CHAPTER FOUR

A Day in the Life

SETTLING IN TOGETHER

PLAYTIME

Life is playfulness. We need to play so that we can discover the magic all around us.

– FLORA COLAO

One of the first objects I remember you reaching for was _____

_____

_____

_____

_____

_____

Your favorite objects to explore were _____

_____

_____

_____

_____

_____

Some of the toys you enjoyed as a baby were

The most chewed toy without a doubt was

Your favorite comfort object was

A toy handed down from another family member was

These are the ways you liked to play

You most enjoyed playing with

You were captivated by _____

You sometimes got frustrated when _____

Playing helped me get to know you because _____

OUT AND ABOUT

There's nothing wrong with having a tree as a friend.

– BOB ROSS

One of the earliest times we went outside was _____

_____

_____

_____

_____

_____

_____

_____

We walked or hiked together by _____

_____

_____

_____

_____

_____

_____

These things in the big outdoors got your attention

The first time you went to the playground was

You loved these outdoor activities

A few stories about the different places we went and the things we did outside when you were a baby

MEALTIMES

You mean to tell me that spoons don't actually sound like airplanes?

– UNKNOWN

As a small baby, you mostly ate _____

_____

_____

_____

_____

You had feeding times _____

_____

_____

_____

Your first solid foods were _____

_____

_____

_____

_____

_____

The foods you liked to stick in your mouth yourself were

Maybe the biggest food mess you ever made was

Your very favorite food was probably

I could tell because

FUNNY FACES

Every happy memory created for a child is another treasure of a lifetime.

– DONNA MARIE

Your favorite silly face was _____

A silly noise you really enjoyed was _____

A song we liked to share was _____

You didn't really like

This is how I felt when you smiled back at me

And your first giggles were

EXPRESSING YOURSELF

A person is a person no matter how small.

– DR. SEUSS

Before you could talk, you communicated with me by

You used to make different noises when you

I could tell you were feeling happy when

You showed me you were hungry by

And I knew you were grumpy when

To cheer you up, I used to

STORYTIME

Books train your imagination to think big.

– TAYLOR SWIFT

Some of your favorite books were _____

_____

_____

_____

_____

_____

_____

We read this book together a thousand times _____

_____

_____

_____

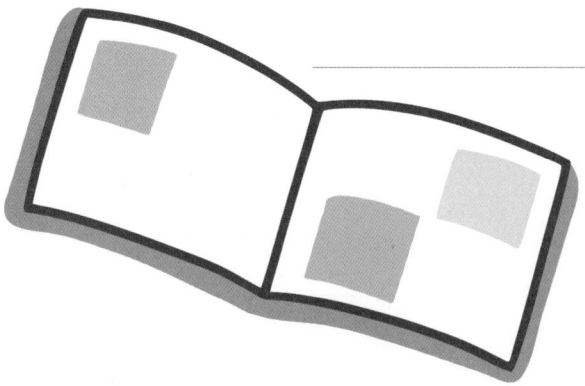

_____

_____

_____

_____

A book you liked to read with someone else was

The character you loved the most was

The pictures and photos in books that got your attention were

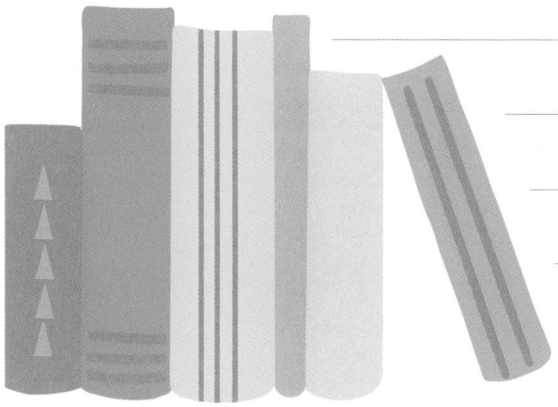

MUSICAL MOMENTS

Music gives a soul to the universe, wings to the mind, flight to the imagination, and life to everything.

– PLATO

You loved to hear these songs over and over _____

_____

_____

_____

_____

Our record for listening to the same song on repeat was _____

_____

_____

_____

_____

Your favorite song with hand motions was _____

_____

_____

_____

_____

The other kinds of music and songs you liked were

The first time you tried to sing along was

A toy musical instrument you loved to play was

SLEEPYTIME

People who say they sleep like a baby usually don't have one.

– UNKNOWN

When you were a baby, you slept like _____

_____

_____

Our bedtime routine was _____

_____

_____

_____

_____

Bathtimes were _____

_____

_____

In the tub you liked to play with _____

_____

_____

_____

The one toy you could never sleep without was _____

_____

_____

_____

_____

And your favorite pair of jammies was _____

_____

_____

_____

_____

_____

Something that made it hard for you to sleep was _____

_____

_____

_____

_____

_____

Something that helped you fall asleep was _____

_____

_____

_____

_____

_____

_____

A letter with love, to remind you of all the ways you made me happy when you were a baby

CHAPTER FIVE

Exploring and Learning

GROWING UP

GETTING AROUND

His little hands stole my heart . . .
and his little feet ran away with it.

– UNKNOWN

This is how I felt when you started to crawl _____

Your favorite place to crawl was _____

A few of your early mishaps

How you learned to walk

You used to make me laugh when

When you started dancing, you moved like

HELLO, YOU

Teaching is listening. Learning is talking.

– DEBORAH MEIER

These are some of the sounds you made before you started talking

Your first word was

The next few words were

Your favorite thing to say was _____

The funniest things you said were _____

You made up words like _____

This is how I felt when I first heard you say my name _____

HAVING FUN

Play is the work of children.

– MARIA MONTESSORI

Once you could walk, the activity you loved the most was _____

A game you liked to play with me was _____

Your favorite thing to do outside was _____

When we went to the park, you made a beeline for the _____

When it was time to stop playing, you _____

PEOPLE IN YOUR WORLD

Love only grows by sharing.

– BRIAN TRACY

Your favorite people were _____

_____

_____

_____

_____

You loved going to see _____

_____

_____

_____

_____

You'd always give a hug or kiss to _____

_____

_____

_____

_____

Someone who babysat you was

A friend or sibling you played alongside was

If no one was around to play, you

IMAGINE THAT

Every child is born blessed with a vivid imagination.

– WALT DISNEY

A few of the stories you made up for us _____

Your favorite things to draw were

Your favorite things to make were

Sometimes it was more fun making a mess, like

You learned to use the computer or tablet when

YOUR FAVORITE THINGS

Children see magic because they look for it.

– CHRISTOPHER MOORE

Once you were a little bit older, your favorite toys were _____

_____

_____

_____

_____

_____

_____

But you didn't give up on _____

_____

_____

_____

_____

_____

_____

If we asked you to name the best thing in your room, it would be

If you could choose your own clothes every single day, you would wear

You liked to dress up as

The sweetest thing you ever made for me was

TREATS AND EATS

You can't buy happiness, but you can buy ice cream, and that is pretty much the same thing.

– UNKNOWN

You loved to eat _____

_____

_____

_____

_____

But you weren't so keen on _____

_____

_____

_____

_____

Something you learned to love was _____

_____

_____

_____

_____

The best breakfast in the world to you was

Your ideal picnic would be

When we went shopping for food, you

The first time you helped out when we were cooking was

CHAPTER SIX

Hopes and Dreams

MY WISHES FOR YOUR FUTURE

LOOKING BACK

Don't look back unless you can smile;
don't look ahead unless you can dream.

– IRISH SAYING

My happiest memory from your early childhood was _____

The hardest part of your early childhood was _____

I'll never forget when

I'll always miss

I was so proud of you when

LOOKING FORWARD

Do not follow where the path may lead. Go instead where there is no path and leave a trail.

– RALPH WALDO EMERSON

I hope to see you grow to become _____

I want you to remember

I know you'll be great at

I'll always be there to

MY MESSAGE TO YOU

My story in this book is finished, but yours is just beginning. Here is a message from me to you, with all my love and wisdom.